GIFTED & TALENTED®

*To develop
your child's gifts
and talents*

Puzzles & Games
for
Reading and Math

Book Two

A Workbook for Ages 6-8

Written by Martha Cheney
Illustrated by Larry Nolte

 Lowell House
Juvenile
Los Angeles

CONTEMPORARY BOOKS
Chicago

Manufactured in the United States of America

ISBN: 1-56565-374-2

10   9   8   7   6   5   4   3

GIFTED & TALENTED® WORKBOOKS will help develop your child's natural talents and gifts by providing activities to enhance critical and creative thinking skills. These skills of logic and reasoning teach children **how** to think. They are precisely the skills emphasized by teachers of gifted and talented children.

Thinking skills are the skills needed to be able to learn anything at any time. Unlike events, words, and teaching methods, thinking skills never change. If a child has a grasp of how to think, school success and even success in life will become more assured. In addition, the child will become self-confident as he or she approaches new tasks with the ability to think them through and discover solutions.

GIFTED & TALENTED® WORKBOOKS present these skills in a unique way, combining the basic subject areas of reading, language arts, and math with thinking skills. The top of each page is labeled to indicate the specific thinking skill developed. Here are some of the skills you will find:

- Deduction—the ability to reach a logical conclusion by interpreting clues

- Understanding Relationships—the ability to recognize how objects, shapes, and words are similar or dissimilar; to classify or categorize

- Sequencing—the ability to organize events, numbers; to recognize patterns

- Inference—the ability to reach a logical conclusion from given or assumed evidence

- Creative Thinking—the ability to generate unique ideas; to compare and contrast the same elements in different situations; to present imaginative solutions to problems

Each book contains activities that challenge children. The activities vary in range from easier to more difficult. You may need to work with your child on many of the pages, especially with the child who is a non-reader. However, even a non-reader can master thinking skills, and the sooner your child learns how to think, the better. Read the directions to your child and, if necessary, explain them. Let your child choose to do the activities that interest him or her. When interest wanes, stop. A page or two at a time may be enough, as the child should have fun while learning.

It is important to remember that these activities are designed to teach your child **how to think**, not how to find the right answer. Teachers of gifted children are never surprised when a child discovers a new "right" answer. For example, a child may be asked to choose the object that doesn't belong in this group: a table, a chair, a book, a desk. The best answer is **book**, since all the others are furniture. But a child could respond that all of them belong because they all could be found in an office or a library. The best way to react to this type of response is to praise the child and gently point out that there is another answer, too. While creativity should be encouraged, your child must look for the best and most **suitable** answer.

GIFTED & TALENTED® WORKBOOKS have been written by teachers. Educationally sound and endorsed by leaders in the gifted field, this series will benefit any child who demonstrates curiosity, imagination, a sense of fun and wonder about the world, and a desire to learn. These books will open your child's mind to new experiences and help fulfill his or her true potential.

Mystery Letter

Each word below can be correctly completed with more than one letter. But you need to find one letter that makes sense in all the words. Add the mystery letter to each word.

ho__se

pai__

sto__y

ove__

__ope

Below, make a list of as many words as you can by using other letters to fill in each blank. Use letters that make sense in each word.

_____   _____

_____   _____

_____   _____

_____   _____

Mystery Letter

Each word below can be correctly completed with more than one letter. But you need to find one letter that makes sense in all the words. Add the mystery letter to each word.

__oad

goa__

__end

rai__

smi__e

Below, make a list of as many words as you can by using other letters to fill in each blank. Use letters that make sense in each word.

_____   _____

_____   _____

_____   _____

_____   _____

Double Mystery Letters

Each word below can be correctly completed with more than one letter. There are two letters that make sense in all the words. Add the mystery letters to each word.

st___r   st___r

r___ng   r___ng

b___g   b___g

w___sh   w___sh

p___ne   p___ne

Below, make a list of as many words as you can by using other letters to fill in each blank. Use letters that make sense in each word.

_____   _____

_____   _____

_____   _____

_____   _____

Ring-a-Round Words

The name of each object pictured below has only three letters. Write the name of one of the objects in any blank space on the ring. Moving clockwise, write another word that is the same as the first one you wrote except for one letter! Continue around the circle until each space is filled with a word that has only one different letter than the words that come before and after it. Use the pictures as clues.

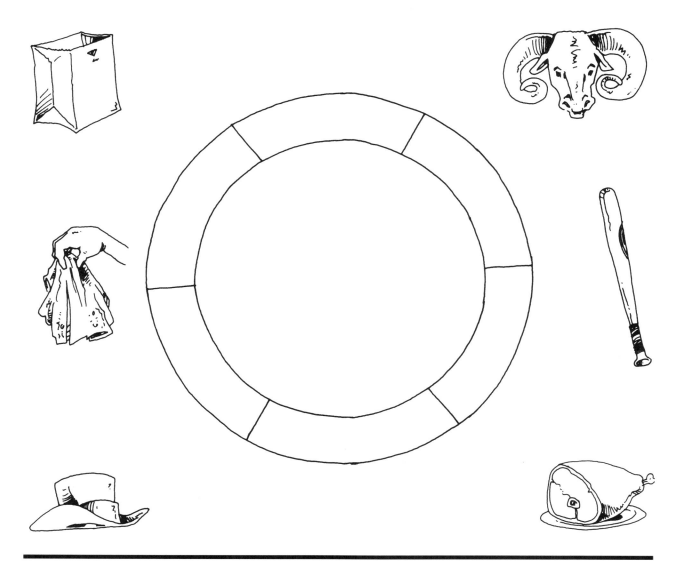

Ring-a-Round Words

The name of each object pictured below has only three letters. Write the name of one of the objects in any blank space on the ring. Moving clockwise, write another word that is the same as the first one you wrote except for one letter! Continue around the circle until each space is filled with a word that has only one different letter than the words that come before and after it. Use the pictures as clues.

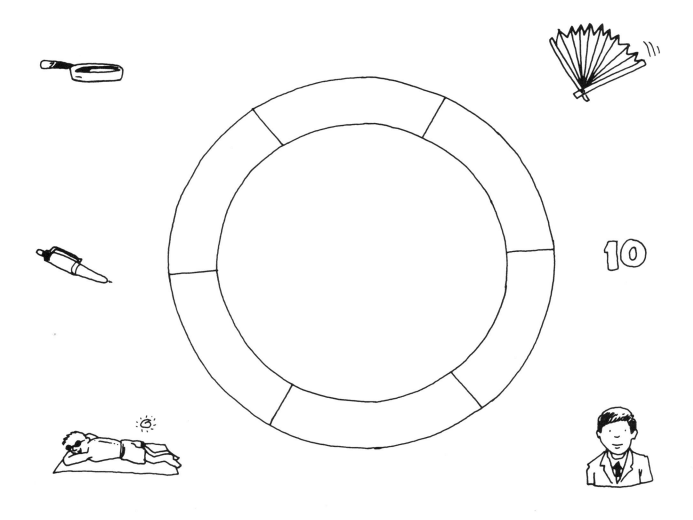

Opposites

Opposites are two things that are as different as they can be. The pictures on this page show some opposites. Write a word beneath each picture to tell what you think the picture means.

_____   _____

_____   _____

Opposites

Opposites are two things that are as different as they can be. The pictures on this page show some opposites. Write a word beneath each picture to tell what you think the picture means.

_____   _____

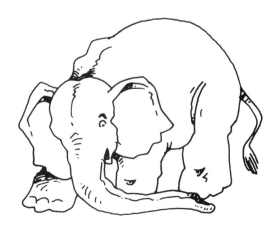

_____   _____

Opposites

Opposites are two things that are as different as they can be. The pictures on this page show some opposites. Write a word beneath each picture to tell what you think the picture means.

_____

_____

_____

_____

Write a Story

Read the story. Draw a line from the story to the picture that shows what the story is about. On the lines at the bottom of the page, write a story that tells about the **other** picture.

Roger is ready to go to school. He has books and a lunch box. He plans to play basketball at recess time.

_____

_____

_____

_____

_____

Write a Story

Read the story. Draw a line from the story to the picture that shows what the story is about. On the lines at the bottom of the page, write a story that tells about the **other** picture.

Marielle is going to make a sandwich. She has bread, peanut butter, jelly, and a knife. She will have a glass of milk with her sandwich.

_____

_____

_____

_____

_____

Finish the Picture

Read the sentences and fill in the blank. Then complete the picture using the information in the sentences to guide you.

Chester the dragon has green scales and sharp nails. He has three spikes on his back. He is holding a _____.

Finish the Picture

Read the sentences and fill in the blank. Then complete the picture using the information in the sentences to guide you.

> Gloria is riding a red surfboard. She is on top of a gigantic wave. A _____ is swimming nearby.

Create Your Own Picture

Make a list of things you would find at a pond. Draw a picture below showing all the things on your list.

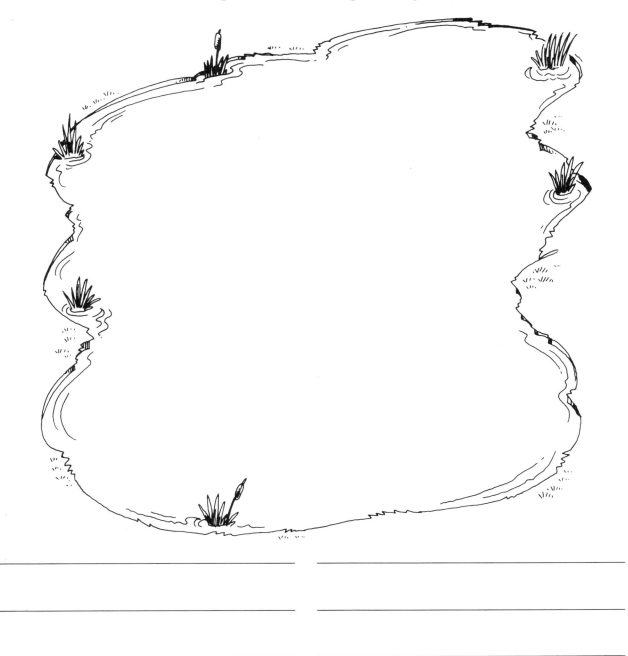

_____ _____

_____ _____

_____ _____

_____ _____

Create Your Own Picture

Make a list of things you would find in a restaurant. Draw a picture below showing all the things on your list.

_____   _____

_____   _____

_____   _____

_____   _____

Compound Words

Each butterfly contains half of a compound word. A **compound word** is made up of two separate words that are joined to become one word. Use the word box at the bottom of the page to find the missing parts of the words. Fill in the butterflies so that each word makes sense.

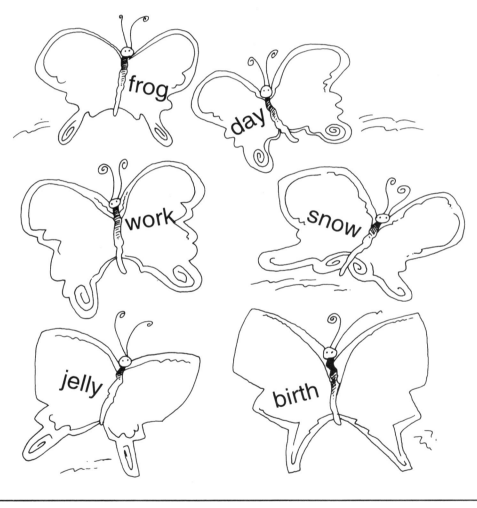

Word Box		
dream	fish	home
bull	day	flake

Compound Words

Each seashell contains half of a compound word. A **compound word** is made up of two separate words that are joined to become one word. Use the word box at the bottom of the page to find the missing parts of the words. Fill in the seashells so that each word makes sense.

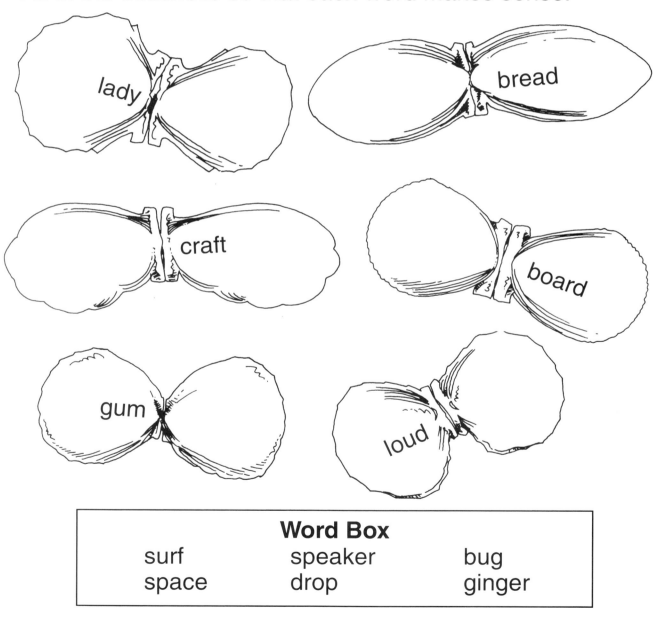

Word Box		
surf	speaker	bug
space	drop	ginger

Scrambled Words

Each word below begins with the letters **m-a-n**. Use the clues to unscramble the words.

Words	**Clues**
ngamo	a tropical fruit
— — — — —	
letnam	a shelf above a fireplace
— — — — — —	
nidonlam	a small stringed instrument
— — — — — — — —	
amicnrue	a treatment for the care of nails
— — — — — — — —	
nasmion	a large and imposing house
— — — — — — —	

Scrambled Words

Each word below begins with the letters **c-a-t**. Use the clues to unscramble the words.

Words	**Clues**
chatc — — — — —	what you do if someone throws you a ball
stupac — — — — — —	a red sauce made from tomatoes
tactle — — — — — —	animals that provide meat and milk
lactait — — — — — — —	a plant with long leaves and fuzzy stalks
caplutat — — — — — — — —	an ancient device used to hurl stones

Scrambled Words

Unscramble the words below. **Hint:** All of the words rhyme!

on   __ __

hughot   __ __ __ __ __ __

wes   __ __ __

ohe   __ __ __

wrog   __ __ __ __

lobwe   __ __ __ __ __

Scrambled Words

Unscramble the words below. **Hint:** One letter appears in the same position in each word.

knuj   __ __ __ __

fnei   __ __ __ __

ntwa   __ __ __ __

ihnt   __ __ __ __

enob   __ __ __ __

grin   __ __ __ __

ntec   __ __ __ __

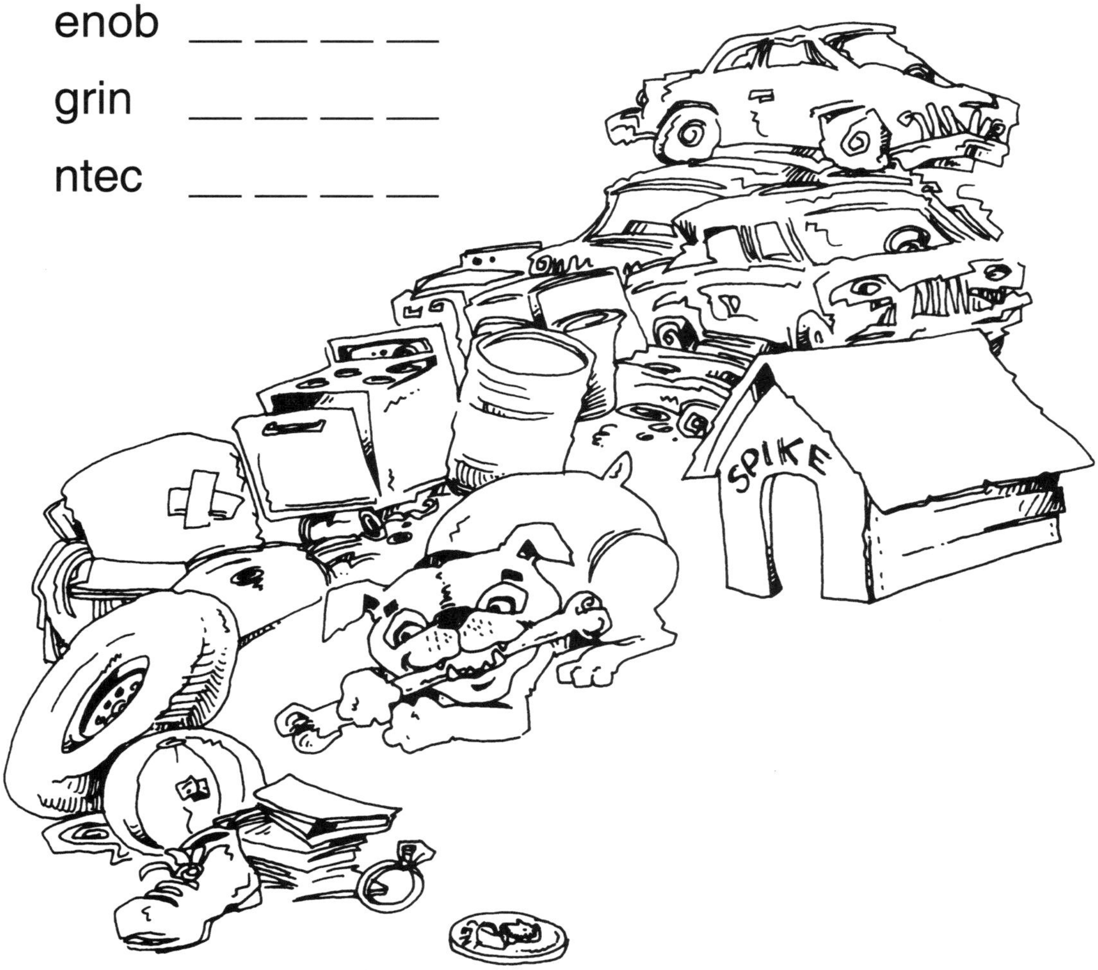

Scrambled Words

Unscramble the words below. **Hint:** One letter appears in the same position in each word.

rsait   __ __ __ __ __

ffreo   __ __ __ __ __

eetrs   __ __ __ __ __

hrece   __ __ __ __ __

priwe   __ __ __ __ __

ramek   __ __ __ __ __

A Rebus Story

In a rebus story, some of the words are replaced by pictures. Read the beginning of this rebus story and complete it using words and pictures.

So the little 🐷

A Rebus Story

In a rebus story, some of the words are replaced by pictures. Read the beginning of this rebus story and complete it using words and pictures.

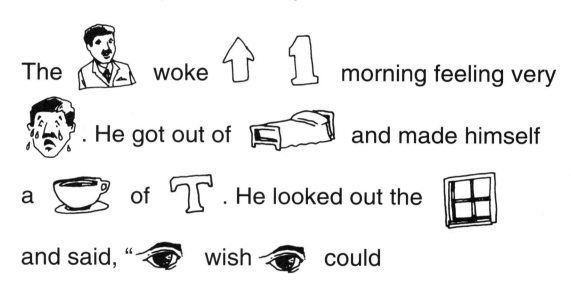

The 🧑 woke ⬆ 1 morning feeling very 😢. He got out of 🛏 and made himself a ☕ of T. He looked out the 🪟 and said, "👁 wish 👁 could

Fractured Words

The picture clues will help you add and subtract parts of words to create new words. Write your answers on the lines. The first one has been done for you.

— an + — b =

man   bug   mug

— at + — st = _____

— ag + — sn + — a = _____

— est + — w + — p = _____

Make up a fractured word puzzle of your own. Challenge a friend or family member to solve it.

Picture/Word Matching

Find and circle each word and picture that means the same, or about the same, as the word **joyful**.

glad

angry

gloomy

happy

cheerful

jolly

Picture/Word Matching

Find and circle each word and picture that means the same, or about the same, as the word **enormous**.

tiny

big

large

giant

little

huge

Sound-Alikes

In each sentence two words are missing. The words are **homonyms,** or words that sound the same, but are spelled differently. Use the picture clues to help you correctly finish each sentence.

My _____ likes to

sit in the _____ .

Oh _____ , the _____

is eating the garden.

Shane _____ his

bike down the _____ .

Adam _____

_____ doughnuts.

Sound-Alikes

In each sentence two words are missing. The words are **homonyms,** or words that sound the same, but are spelled differently. Use the picture clues to help you correctly finish each sentence.

The wind _____ the

_____ kite high in the air.

Andrew _____

the football _____

the target.

Rachel _____ the book

with the _____ cover.

Matt _____ he had

to take care of his

_____ car.

What Do They Like?

Read the clues to find out what each child likes. Complete the last sentence in each group with a phrase that explains how the things the child likes are all alike.

Janine likes soup, but not ice cream.
She likes summer, but not winter.
She likes sweaters, but not shorts.

Janine likes _____ .

Ricardo likes numbers, but not letters.
He likes newspapers, but not magazines.
He likes nuts, but not pretzels.

Ricardo likes _____ .

Jennifer likes snow, but not ice.
She likes cotton, but not cardboard.
She likes bananas, but not apples.

Jennifer likes _____ .

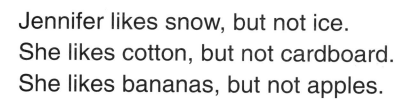

Drawing Conclusions

Read each pair of statements. Write a conclusion based on what you read about each pair. The first one has been done for you.

Nurntuckets are wild.
All wild things are furry.

Conclusion: <u>Nurntuckets are furry</u>.

Billswoggles are green.
All green things are alive.

Conclusion: _____ .

Merklets are sweet.
All sweet things are sticky.

Conclusion: _____ .

Floogles are blubbery.
All blubbery things live in the sea.

Conclusion: _____ .

On another sheet of paper, make up your own pairs of statements. Challenge a friend or family member to read each of your statements and write a conclusion.

A Birthday Puzzle

Mrs. Hamilton's children are growing up so fast that she sometimes has difficulty remembering their ages and birthdays. Use the clues below to help her remember. Fill in the chart as you discover information contained in the clues. You may have to read the clues several times, adding new information to the chart each time.

- The boy who was born in June is 7 years old.
- Doug is not 4 years old.
- Gordon is older than Meg.
- One of the children was born in September, but it was not Gordon.
- Meg's birthday is in April.
- The youngest child is only 2 years old.

	Name	Age	Birthday Month
Oldest			
Middle			
Youngest			

A Family Tradition

The Brandts, the Smarts, and the Pattersons each have a family tradition of getting together for Sunday dinner. Each family serves a special meal at a certain time of day. Each family has a particular set of china used only for this meal. Use the clues below to find out about each family's Sunday dinner. Fill in the chart below as you discover information contained in the clues. You may have to read the clues several times, adding new information each time.

- The Smart family eats at noon.
- The family that serves fried chicken uses blue china.
- The Brandt family eats at two o'clock.
- The family that serves spaghetti does not use red china.
- The family that eats at one o'clock serves fried chicken.
- The Patterson family does not use white china.
- The family that eats latest likes meatloaf.

	Food	Time	Color of China
Brandts			
Smarts			
Pattersons			

Winter Sports

Heather, Jacquie, and Kerri are best friends. The girls all like winter sports. Use the clues below to find out what sports and games the girls like best, and how they like their hot chocolate! Fill in the chart below as you discover information contained in the clues. You may have to read the clues several times, adding new information to the chart each time.

- Neither Kerri nor Jacquie likes to ski.
- The girl who likes to skate also likes to play Monopoly.
- Heather does not like a marshmallow in her hot chocolate.
- The girl who likes to snowboard likes whipped cream in her hot chocolate.
- Kerri does not like to play cards.
- Jacquie does not like to snowboard.
- Heather does not like to play Scrabble.

	Sport	Game	Hot Chocolate
Heather			
Kerri			
Jacquie			

Math Club

The Pet Show

There were many wonderful pets entered in the school pet show, but Travis, Emma, and Sena won the top prizes. Use the clues below to find out about the pets and the order in which they placed. Fill in the chart below as you discover information contained in the clues. You may have to read the clues several times, adding new information to the chart each time.

- One of the pets was named Bernie.
- Travis did not come in first.
- Sena's pet was named Bingo.
- Emma did not have a hedgehog.
- The iguana took third place.
- The iguana did not belong to Travis.
- The parrot did not come in first.
- Emma's pet was not named Buster.

	Child's Name	Type of Pet	Pet's Name
First Place			
Second Place			
Third Place			

Shoot for a Star

Begin at the sign that says **Start**. Move from a number to a plus or minus sign, then to another number. Continue, alternating numbers and signs. You can move horizontally or vertically, but not diagonally. Find a pathway to the answer, which is marked with a star. There are several other pathways that lead to the answer. Can you find some of them?

Start

4	+	1	−	2	−
+	3	−	3	+	5
1	+	4	−	2	−
+	2	−	5	+	1
5	−	1	+	4	−
+	3	−	4	+	2

= 10

Help the Hungry Bunny

Begin at the sign that says **Start**. Move from a number to a plus or minus sign, then to another number. Continue, alternating numbers and signs. You can move horizontally or vertically, but not diagonally. Find a pathway to the answer, which is marked with a carrot. There are several other pathways that lead to the answer. Can you find some of them?

Start

4	–	3	–	1	+
+	5	+	2	+	4
3	–	6	–	1	–
+	2	–	3	–	5
6	+	2	–	4	+
–	5	+	6	–	3

= 0

Dive for Sunken Treasure

Begin at the sign that says **Start**. Move from a number to a plus or minus sign, then to another number. Continue, alternating numbers and signs. You can move horizontally or vertically, but not diagonally. Find a pathway to the answer, which is marked with a treasure chest. There are several other pathways that lead to the answer. Can you find some of them?

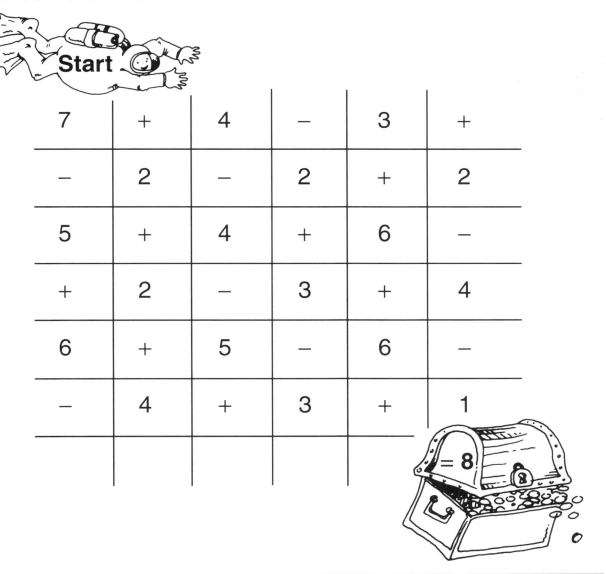

7	+	4	−	3	+
−	2	−	2	+	2
5	+	4	+	6	−
+	2	−	3	+	4
6	+	5	−	6	−
−	4	+	3	+	1

= 8

Amazing Patterns

To find the correct path from **Start** to **Finish** you must first determine what the pattern is. Read each pathway pattern carefully. Mark each error in the pattern with an **X**. An **X** means that the pathway is blocked and cannot be used. When you have found all the errors, there will be only one pathway left open!

Shape Tic-Tac-Toe

Instead of **X**'s and **O**'s, this tic-tac-toe game uses triangles and squares! To play the game you must know how to find a sum. A **sum** is the answer to any addition problem. Follow the instructions below.

- Place a triangle on the sum of 6 + 6.
- Place a square on the sum of 8 + 5.
- Place a triangle on the sum of 9 + 9.
- Place a square on the sum of 7 + 2.
- Place a triangle on the sum of 5 + 6.
- Place a square on the sum of 6 + 9.
- Place a triangle on the sum of 3 + 7.
- Place a square on the sum of 5 + 3.

Did triangle or square win the game? _____

14	9	18
15	12	11
13	8	10

Create Your Own Tic-Tac-Toe Game

Fill in the grid below with sums. A **sum** is the answer to any addition problem. Use **X**'s and **O**'s to play the game. Write a set of directions that will make **X** win the game!

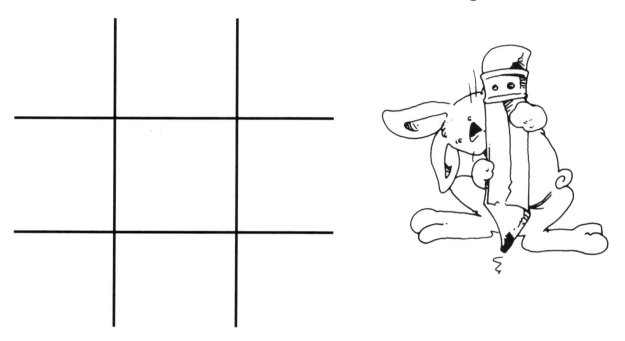

- Place an **X** on the sum of _____.
- Place an **O** on the sum of _____.
- Place an **X** on the sum of _____.
- Place an **O** on the sum of _____.
- Place an **X** on the sum of _____.
- Place an **O** on the sum of _____.
- Place an **X** on the sum of _____.
- Place an **O** on the sum of _____.
- Place an **X** on the sum of _____.

Space Tic-Tac-Toe

Instead of **X**'s and **O**'s, this tic-tac-toe game uses stars and moons. To play this game you must know how to find a product. A **product** is the answer to any multiplication problem. Follow the instructions below.

- Place a star on the product of 9 × 2.
- Place a moon on the product of 5 × 5.
- Place a star on the product of 7 × 3.
- Place a moon on the product of 6 × 4.
- Place a star on the product of 3 × 9.
- Place a moon on the product of 4 × 7.
- Place a star on the product of 4 × 4.
- Place a moon on the product of 6 × 5.
- Place a star on the product of 5 × 4.

Did star or moon win the game? _____

28	27	21
16	24	20
25	18	30

Create Your Own Tic-Tac-Toe Game

Fill in the grid below with products. A **product** is the answer to any multiplication problem. Use **X**'s and **O**'s to play the game. Write a set of directions that will make **O** win the game!

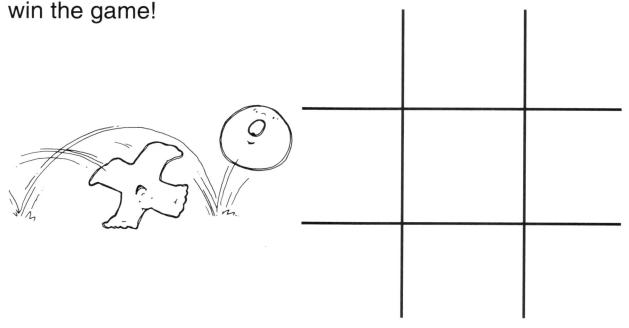

- Place an **O** on the product of _____.
- Place an **X** on the product of _____.
- Place an **O** on the product of _____.
- Place an **X** on the product of _____.
- Place an **O** on the product of _____.
- Place an **X** on the product of _____.
- Place an **O** on the product of _____.
- Place an **X** on the product of _____.
- Place an **O** on the product of _____.

Charlie's Chickens

Charlie's baby chicks have just hatched and they are running all over the henhouse. Look at the page and guess how many chicks there are. This is called an **estimate**.

Write your estimate on the line. _____

Now count the chicks, circling each group of ten.

How many chicks does Charlie really have?_____

How close was your estimate? Subtract the smaller number from the larger number to find out.

The Snowy Mountains

How much snow did the Snowy Mountains get during the winter months? Read the information below to find out. Use crayons to shade in the graph.

- It snowed 1 inch on December 19.
- It snowed 6 inches on December 24.
- It snowed 4 inches on January 8.
- It snowed 2 inches on January 12.
- It snowed 1 inch on January 16.
- It snowed 1 inch on January 25.
- It snowed 5 inches on January 30.
- It snowed 3 inches on February 2.
- It snowed 5 inches on February 10.
- It snowed 2 inches on February 18.
- It snowed 4 inches on February 27.

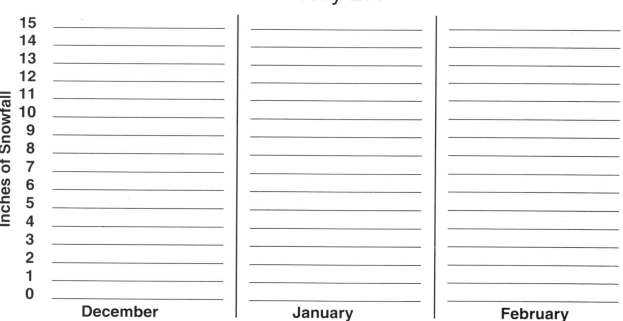

In which month did it snow the most? _____

How Many Ways?

Think about **12**.

Here are several different ways to describe the number **12**:

6 + 6

14 − 2

one dozen

3 × 4

The hours of noon and midnight.

60 ÷ 5

Think of more ways to describe this number. You may use words and pictures.

_____

_____

_____

_____

_____

_____

How Many Ways?

Think about **10**.

Here are several different ways to describe the number **10**:

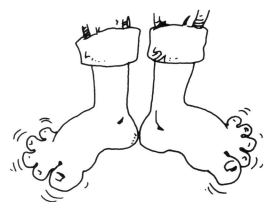

5 + 5

30 − 20

5 × 2

The number of cents in a dime.

Think of more ways to describe
this number. You may use words and pictures.

_____

_____

_____

_____

_____

_____

_____

How Many Ways?

Think about **30**.

Here are several different ways to describe the number **30**:

6×5

The number of days in September.

$10 + 10 + 10$

The number of ears on 15 elephants.

Think of more ways to describe
this number. You may use words and pictures.

_____

_____

_____

_____

_____

_____

_____

How Many Ways?

Think about **4**.

How many ways can you think of to describe the number **4**? You may use words and pictures.

_____

_____

_____

_____

Pick your favorite number.
Write it in the box.

How many ways can you think of to describe your favorite number? You may use words and pictures.

_____

_____

_____

_____

Area

Area refers to the amount of space that is included within a set of lines. You can find the area of the figures on this page by counting the squares inside of each figure. Count two half squares as one whole square.

Hint: Imagine that each square = 1 square foot

What is the area of the triangle?_____

What is the area of the rectangle?_____

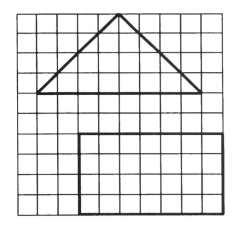
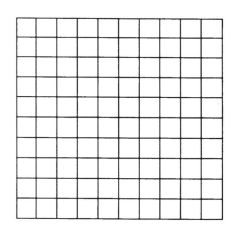

In the empty grid, draw a different figure that has the same area as the rectangle.

Area

Draw as many figures as you can that have an area of 12 square feet.

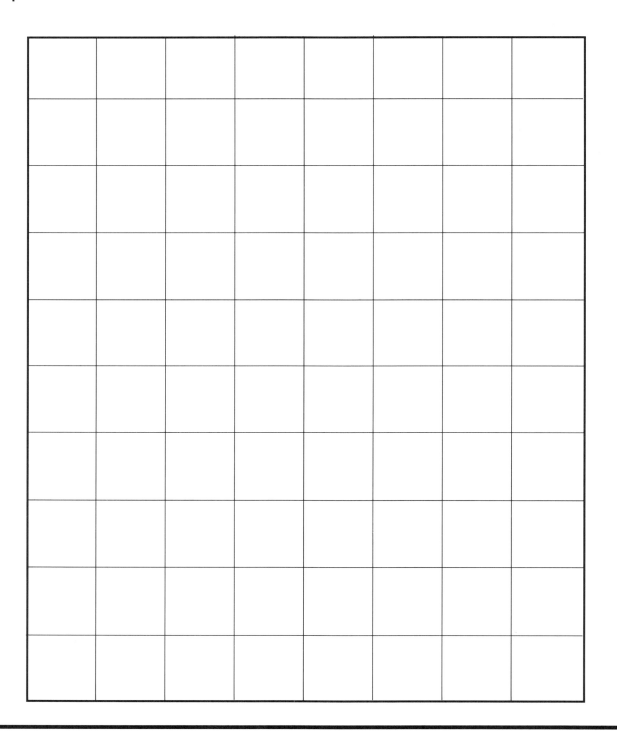

Shape Search

Answer the questions below about the shapes in the box.

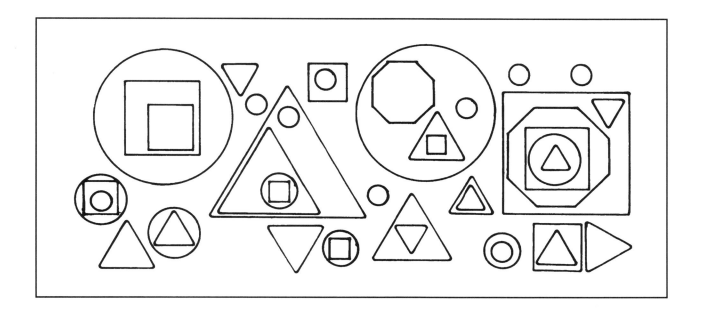

How many squares are inside circles?_____

How many squares are not inside circles?_____

How many squares are there?_____

How many octagons are there?_____

How many triangles are inside other triangles?_____

How many triangles are inside circles?_____

How many triangles are there? _____

How many circles are there?_____

Follow the Dots

Continue each pattern. **Hint:** It may help to count the dots!

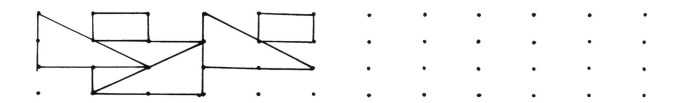

Follow the Dots

Continue each pattern. **Hint:** It may help to count the dots!

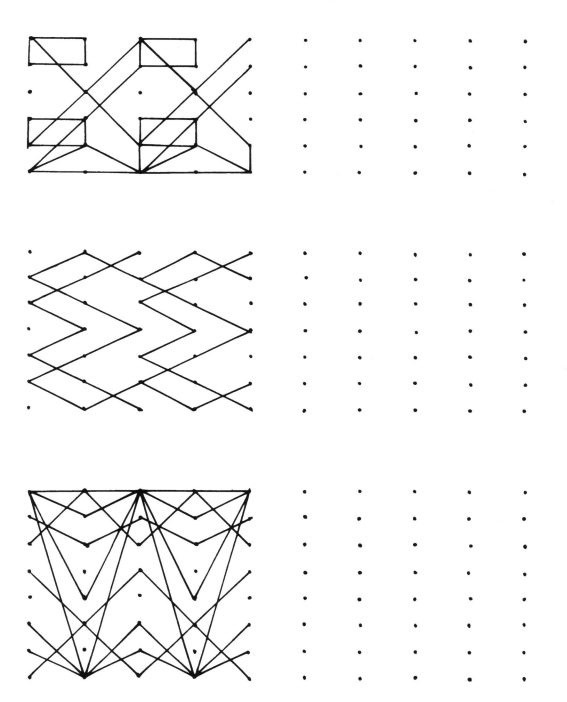

Number Patterns

How is each top number changed to become the number below it? In each little box write a plus or a minus sign to show whether something is added or taken away. Then fill in the missing numbers. In the last four problems you need to fill in **both** missing numbers!

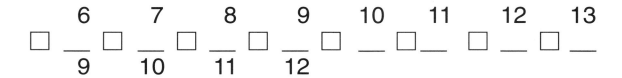

A Doggone Mystery

While Mr. Burton had his back turned, a dog ran into his butcher shop, snatched a steak off the counter, and ran out the back door. Mr. Burton was mad! He asked three other shopkeepers to describe the dog. The shopkeepers really didn't want to help Mr. Burton find the dog, so they each told him something about the dog that was true, and something that was false. Using their clues, circle the picture of the guilty dog.

- Shopkeeper Number 1 said: "The dog had black hair and a long tail."

- Shopkeeper Number 2 said: "The dog had a short tail and wore a collar."

- Shopkeeper Number 3 said: "The dog had white hair and no collar."

Answers

Answers

Page 5
The letter is r.
Rest of answers will vary.

Page 6
The letter is l.
Rest of answers will vary.

Page 7
The letters are a and i.
Rest of answers will vary.

Page 8
Sequence can start anywhere on circle: bag, bat, hat, ham, ram, rag

Page 9
Sequence can start anywhere on circle: man, pan, fan, tan, ten, pen

Page 10
Answers will vary but may include:

high	low
up	down
jump	fall
hot	cold
summer	winter

Page 11
Answers will vary but may include:

happy	sad
laugh	cry
large	small
big	little

Page 12
Answers will vary but may include:

dirty	clean
messy	neat
greedy	generous
kind	unkind

Page 13

Roger is ready to go to school. He has books and a lunch box. He plans to play basketball at recess time.

Page 14

Marielle is going to make a sandwich. She has bread, peanut butter, jelly, and a knife. She will have a glass of milk with her sandwich.

Page 15
Parent: Picture should reflect child's understanding of text.

Page 16
Parent: Picture should reflect child's understanding of text.

Page 17
Answers will vary but may include:
fish, turtle, mud, water, dragonfly, spider, boat, beaver, fisherman, birds, reeds, water lilies

Page 18
Answers will vary but may include:
stove, refrigerator, microwave, tables, chairs, telephone, dishes, pots and pans, food, napkins, tablecloths

Page 19
bullfrog
daydream
homework
snowflake
jellyfish
birthday

Page 20
ladybug
gingerbread
spacecraft
surfboard
gumdrop
loudspeaker

Page 21
mango
mantel
mandolin
manicure
mansion

Page 22
catch
catsup
cattle
cattail
catapult

Page 23
no
though
sew
hoe
grow
below

Page 24
junk
fine
want
hint
bone
ring
cent

Page 25
stair
offer
steer
wiper
maker

Page 26
Once upon a time a little pig lived in a big barn. "I like this barn," said the little pig, "but I would like to see more of the world." So the little pig . . .
Rest of answer will vary.

Page 27
The man woke up one morning feeling very sad. He got out of bed and made himself a cup of tea. He looked out the window and said, "I wish I could . . ."
Rest of answer will vary.

Page 28
car
flower
chicken

Page 29

Page 30

Page 31
son, sun
dear, deer
rode, road
ate, eight

Page 32
blew, blue
threw, through
read, red
knew, new

Page 33
things that are warm
things that start with **N**
things that are soft

Page 34
Billswoggles are alive.
Merklets are sticky.
Floogles live in the sea.

Page 35
Gordon	7	June
Meg	4	April
Doug	2	September

Page 36
meatloaf	2	red
spaghetti	12	white
fried chicken	1	blue

Page 37
Heather   skiing   cards   plain
Kerri   snowboarding
        Scrabble   cream
Jacquie   skating   Monopoly
    marshmallow

Page 38
Sena	hedgehog	Bingo
Travis	parrot	Buster
Emma	iguana	Bernie

Page 39

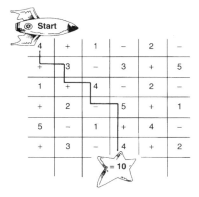

One solution is shown. There are other possibilities.

Page 40

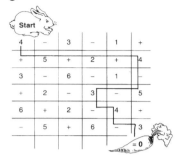

One solution is shown. There are other possibilities.

Page 41

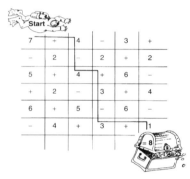

One solution is shown. There are other possibilities.

Page 42

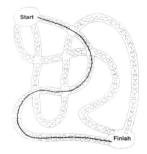

Page 43

Triangle won the game.

Page 44
Answers will vary.

Page 45

Moon won the game.

Page 46
Answers will vary.

Page 47
Estimates will vary. The exact number is 60.

Page 48

It snowed the most in February.

Page 49
Answers will vary.

Page 50
Answers will vary.

Page 51
Answers will vary.

Page 52
Answers will vary.

Page 53
Area of the triangle: 16 square feet
Area of the rectangle: 28 square feet
Rest of answer will vary.

Page 54
Answers will vary.

Page 55
Squares inside circles: 6
Squares not inside circles: 4
Squares: 10
Octagons: 2
Triangles inside triangles: 3
Triangles inside circle: 2
Triangles: 13
Circles: 16

Page 56
Parent: Each design should be correctly continued across the page.

Page 57
Parent: Each design should be correctly continued across the page.

Page 58
+3 each time. Missing numbers are: 13, 14, 15, 16.
−5 each time. Missing numbers are: 20, 25, 30, 35.

Page 59
Since we know that one statement in each pair is true and one is false, we can rule out any dog about whom both parts of the statement are true. Also, we can rule out any dog about whom both parts of the statement are false. This leaves only the dog with black hair, a short tail, and no collar.

Other

books that will help develop your child's gifts and talents

Workbooks:
- Reading (4-6) $3.95
- Math (4-6) $3.95
- Language Arts (4-6) $3.95
- Puzzles & Games for
  Reading and Math (4-6) $3.95
- Puzzles & Games for
  Critical and Creative Thinking (4-6) $3.95
- Reading Book Two (4-6) $3.95
- Math Book Two (4-6) $3.95
- Phonics (4-6) $4.95
- Reading (6-8) $3.95
- Math (6-8) $3.95
- Language Arts (6-8) $3.95
- Puzzles & Games for
  Reading and Math (6-8) $3.95
- Puzzles & Games for
  Critical and Creative Thinking (6-8) $3.95
- Puzzles & Games for
  Reading and Math, Book Two (6-8) $3.95
- Phonics (6-8) $4.95

Reference Workbooks:
- Word Book (4-6) $3.95
- Almanac (6-8) $3.95

Over 6 million sold!

- Atlas (6-8) $3.95
- Dictionary (6-8) $3.95

Story Starters:
- My First Stories (6-8) $3.95
- Stories About Me (6-8) $3.95

Question & Answer Books:
- The Gifted & Talented® Question & Answer
  Book for Ages 4-6 $5.95
- The Gifted & Talented® Question & Answer
  Book for Ages 6-8 $5.95

Drawing Books:
- Learn to Draw (6 and up) $5.95

Readers:
- Double the Trouble (6-8) $7.95
- Time for Bed (6-8) $7.95

For Parents:
- How to Develop Your Child's Gifts and
  Talents During the Elementary Years $11.95
- How to Develop Your Child's Gifts and
  Talents in Math $12.95
- How to Develop Your Child's Gifts and
  Talents in Reading $12.95

....

Available where good books are sold! **or** *Send a check or money order, plus shipping charges, to:*

Department JH
Lowell House
2029 Century Park East, Suite 3290
Los Angeles, CA 90067

For special or bulk sales, call (800) 552-7551, EXT 112

Handy Worksheet

Note: Minimum order of three titles. ***On a separate piece of paper,***
please specify exact titles and ages and include a breakdown of costs, as follows:

....

(# of books) _____ x **$3.95** = _____	**(Subtotal)**	= _____
(# of books) _____ x **$4.95** = _____	*California residents*	
(# of books) _____ x **$5.95** = _____	*add 8.25% sales tax*	= _____
(# of books) _____ x **$7.95** = _____	**Shipping charges**	
(# of books) _____ x **$11.95** = _____	*(# of books)* ____ x **$1.00/ book**	= _____
(# of books) _____ x **$12.95** = _____	***Total cost***	= _____